GREEN MATTERS™

Making Good Choices About
RENEWABLE RESOURCES

JEANNE NAGLE

rosen publishing's
rosen
central®

New York

For future generations of my family and families everywhere

Published in 2010 by The Rosen Publishing Group, Inc.
29 East 21st Street, New York, NY 10010

Library of Congress Cataloging-in-Publication Data

Nagle, Jeanne.
Making good choices about renewable resources / Jeanne Nagle.—1st ed.
    p. cm.—(Green matters)
Includes bibliographical references and index.
ISBN-13: 978-1-4358-5310-2 (library binding)
ISBN-13: 978-1-4358-5602-8 (pbk)
ISBN-13: 978-1-4358-5603-5 (6 pack)
1. Conservation of natural resources—Juvenile literature. 2. Sustainable living—Juvenile literature. 3. Renewable natural resources—Juvenile literature. I. Title.
S940.N34 2010
333.72—dc22
                                                                    2008049318

Manufactured in Malaysia

CONTENTS

INTRODUCTION

Earth is very kind to its inhabitants. The planet provides many natural resources, which are materials found in nature that support basic human needs. Animals and plants, drinkable water, oxygen-rich air, and the wood from trees that is used for shelter—for building houses—are all natural resources. So are the oil and coal that heat those homes, cook the food, and make people more comfortable. But, actually, those last two items are a different kind of resource. Oil and coal are what's known as nonrenewable resources. The others mentioned are renewable.

Something is renewed when it comes back to its original form or better, basically when it is made new again. Whether or not a particular natural resource is considered renewable depends on what happens after an original supply of materials is consumed, or used. In the case of oil and coal, there is only so much to go around. The supply is limited. Once it is used up, it cannot, for all practical purposes, be made new again.

Renewable resources, on the other hand, can be naturally replenished, or stocked up again. Take the examples given earlier. Animals reproduce, meaning they have babies. The newborns grow up and take the place of those that have gone before. Likewise, vegetables and fruits release their seeds so that additional produce can grow. Water renews itself through a cycle in which moisture collected on the ground evaporates into the air and then comes back as rain or snow, refilling the lakes and streams that provide drinking water. Trees and plants filter carbon dioxide and other pollutants out of the air, leaving living organisms with fresh oxygen to breathe. Forests renew themselves by

growing new trees from seeds, replacing those that have fallen or been cut down for construction and other uses.

Renewing natural resources takes time, however. For instance, it takes months for new populations of animals and plants to grow, and years for forests to develop trees mature enough for usable lumber. Consequently, consuming renewable resources too quickly either lessens or completely destroys their ability to regenerate and replenish themselves. This effect threatens the available supply of resources that humans depend on for their survival. So, even though renewable resources are limitless in theory, there is a chance that they could become temporarily, or even permanently, nonrenewable because of misuse.

When you consider all the facts, two concepts become obvious. Humans should use more renewable resources than nonrenewable ones whenever possible because there's a stronger, regenerating supply of renewable materials. Just as important, people should handle Earth's renewable resources with great care in order to ensure that they aren't overused and don't lose their valuable support. Achieving these goals requires thinking ahead, cooperation, and hard work. But humans owe it to themselves to secure the health of their generous, life-sustaining planet and its natural resources. Understanding the vital role that renewable resources play in people's lives, and making smart choices regarding their use, is the responsibility of every individual—starting with you.

The Lowdown on Renewable Energy

The hottest topic in any discussion of natural resources is energy use. As the source of motion and activity, energy is such an important part of everyday life. After all, modern society depends heavily on technology. The machines, tools, and equipment that make doing business easier and recreation more fun cannot work without energy or power.

Currently, most of that power comes from nonrenewable sources. Yet, there are choices where energy is concerned. Natural, renewable sources of power are available, although they are not widely used in the United States. Only about 6 percent of energy consumed in the United States is from renewable resources. Still, alternative energy is gaining in popularity in America and other developed nations. As the cost of nonrenewable fossil fuels rises, the supply shrinks and the fuels' harmful effect on the environment becomes more apparent.

Utility companies collect solar power using row upon row of reflective collectors. Several collectors grouped together can generate enough electricity to power a town.

THE POWER OF THE SUN

When searching for a powerful and reliable source of renewable energy, all humans need to do is look to the sky. Each second, the sun releases enough energy to equal nearly 3 quintillion gallons (11.4 quintillion liters) of gasoline. (That's a three followed by eighteen zeros.) Earth actually absorbs only a tiny fraction of that energy, but it is enough to heat the planet and encourage plants and food crops to grow. Rays from the sun also provide enough solar energy to heat buildings and water tanks, as well as power any number of electrical appliances and gadgets.

Solar energy is considered either passive or active. Passive solar energy takes advantage of the sun's natural properties, light and heat, to directly regulate temperatures and generate electricity. Passive solar energy starts with sunlight entering an enclosed space, such as a house or office, through the glass in windows and skylights. The natural glow from the sun that lights up a space is a form of passive solar energy called daylighting.

Once inside, the sun's rays are also converted to heat, which cannot penetrate back through the glass. So, it gets trapped inside the space. A buildup of solar heat raises temperatures, resulting in passive solar heating. Passive solar cooling occurs when sunlight is blocked from reaching the space.

These days, all sorts of electronics, such as cell phones, are being built to use power gathered from small, personal solar collectors.

Mechanical devices are needed to tap and store active solar energy. Photovoltaic cells, such as the glass-covered disks or strips on remote-controlled toys or groups of larger cells in panels placed on rooftops, are the most familiar active solar energy collectors. Made of silicon, solar cells absorb sunlight, which reacts with the silicon to generate electricity. Metal wires move electrical current from cells into electronic devices.

Other forms of active solar collection use heat and steam to generate power. Parabolic troughs are long, curved rectangles that are lined with mirrors. A trough reflects sunlight so that it heats fluid flowing along its center. The fluid is converted to steam, which powers a turbine engine. Solar dishes work pretty much the same way—only they are larger than troughs and are rounded like a satellite dish. Tower power is generated when the sun's rays warm fluid that is held in mirrored tanks that sit on top of tall receiving towers. Solar towers are built primarily for commercial use. Pilot program towers had been in operation in California until 1999, and Spain began operating a commercial tower in 2007. Other solar power towers are in development in South Africa and the United States, in Southern California.

THE MIGHTY WIND

Harnessing the wind as a power source is not a new concept. Windmills have been around for centuries in Europe, used to power machinery that would grind corn and grain into flour. Today, wind energy is used worldwide to generate electricity. Skinnier, more efficient collection devices known as wind turbines have replaced windmills.

A turbine is a machine or motor that creates electricity using kinetics, or movement by force. Wind is the force that moves a wind turbine's blades, also called the rotor. The rotor can be either horizontal—the most common type, which looks like a fan or a traditional windmill—or vertical, twisting around from top to bottom like a giant

Whether their rotors are horizontal *(left)* or vertical *(below)*, modern turbines are much sleeker in design than old-fashioned windmills.

egg beater. The rotating blades spin a mechanical shaft inside the turbine, which is attached to a generator that creates electricity.

Wind turbines come in small, medium, and large sizes. Typically, one small turbine has a rotor anywhere from 4 feet (1.25 meters) to 29 feet (8.8 m) in diameter. It generates enough electricity to power a single-family household. Medium and large turbines are the kind that you see gathered together on a wind farm. They have huge rotors, ranging anywhere from 30 to 50 feet (10 to 15 m), all the way up to 200 feet (60 m). The larger the rotor, the more electricity is produced. Neighborhoods, or even entire communities, can get their electricity from wind farms.

HYDROPOWER

Kinetics also come into play with the largest source of renewable energy in the United States—water. Instead of wind, flowing currents of water from streams and rivers push the blades of wheels called water turbines. The spinning blades turn the shaft of a generator and create energy called hydroelectricity.

In the past, hydropower was collected through water wheels that only turned as fast as a river's natural current. Water wheel energy was enough to turn shafts that powered machinery in mills that produced flour or cut trees into lumber. However, as the demand for hydropower grew, dams were built to control—and thereby increase—the force of the water flow. Damming the flow of water creates a waterfall, and falling water has more force. By placing turbines at the base of the dams and connecting generators directly to those turbines, people were able to collect greater amounts of electricity.

Producing electricity by means of dams and generator-driven power plants, called impoundment, is still the most common hydropower col- lection method used today. Another is diversion, in which swiftly flowing river water is rerouted into a specially dug canal. The canal water is then run through turbines connected to a generator.

HYDROPOWER-FUL NATIONS

In 1882, the world's first hydroelectric power plant opened in Appleton, Wisconsin. The plant consisted of a dam on the Fox River, a turbine built into the dam, and a power station. Within four years, more than forty similar plants had begun service in the United States and Canada.

Today, approximately 10 percent of electricity consumed in the United States comes from hydropower, according to the U.S. Department of Energy. The Canadian government reports that two-thirds of the country's electricity is hydroelectricity. In fact, Canada is the world's largest producer (and second-largest exporter) of hydroelectricity.

Covering about three-quarters of Earth's surface, oceans also have the potential to be a virtually limitless source of renewable hydropower. Energy exists in the kinetic motion of waves and ocean tides, as well as solar heat absorbed by seawater. Collecting that energy, however, can be tough. Current collection technologies are experimental and expensive, delivering only small amounts of power. Scientists continue to work on systems that will make oceans an affordable, convenient, and reliable alternative energy source.

GEOTHERMAL ENERGY

Have you ever seen a geyser, such as Old Faithful at Yellowstone National Park, blow steam and hot water sky-high? Or maybe you've

Steam and long lengths of pipe, such as these at the Wairakei Geothermal Power Station in New Zealand, indicate the area where geothermal power plants are in full "on" mode.

watched video footage of a volcano as it spewed fiery lava. If so, then you've witnessed geothermal energy in action.

Geothermal energy comes from heat that is inside Earth's many layers. According to the U.S. Department of Energy, the planet's center, or core, produces more heat than can be found on the surface of the sun. Rocks and water are warmed by the superheated core all the way through to the crust, which is Earth's outermost layer. Sometimes, heat breaks through the crust in the form of geyser steam or the melted rocks that make up lava. Pools of heated water called hot springs also appear on or near the planet's surface. Water from hot springs can be run through pipes and used to heat buildings.

Wood chips and other biomass materials get loaded by the truckload and burned to create organic biopower in Ichihara, Japan.

The majority of Earth's warmth, though, remains underground. Therefore, tapping geothermal heat usually requires some digging. Just 10 feet (about 3 m) below the surface, ground temperatures are a fairly steady 50 or 60 degrees Fahrenheit (10 to 15.5 degrees Celsius). Tubes containing water are placed underground at that depth and looped back up to a condenser. The water in the tubes absorbs the stable ground heat and is run through a condenser, which uses pressure to turn the heated water into a vapor. The vapor is pumped into a building as heat. To cool a building, warm air is pumped back into the ground.

Heated earth can also generate electricity through what's known as geothermal power plants. Underground pipes collect naturally heated water and steam, which is then funneled through a turbine. As with hydropower and wind power, the turbine turns a shaft that is connected to a generator, which creates electricity.

BIOMASS

When they are eaten, plants provide nutrition, which is a power source for the human body. But that is not the only type of energy that comes from vegetation. Biomass, which is the scientific name for organic plant material and waste matter, can generate heat and electricity as well.

Burning firewood and other tree products or parts, such as wood chips, leaves, or bark, is the most common form of generating biomass heat. Used today in the same way it has been used for centuries, bioheat warms homes and cooks food. Burning biomass also assists in the production of biopower. Steam from water heated by plant material, including wood, turns a turbine to generate electricity.

Biopower also comes from plant life that is dead or dying. When vegetation dies, it releases a gas called methane. Rather than have methane poison the air, biopower companies collect it from sources like landfills and farms. The gas travels through pipes buried in the layers of dirt and waste of a landfill, is filtered and compressed (squeezed together), and is then used as fuel to power an electricity-producing generator. Anaerobic digesters are air-tight tanks filled with bacteria that eat organic farm waste—usually manure—and produce methane. Trapped in the tanks, the methane is piped into a generator and is converted into electricity.

Biomass is a key ingredient in biofuel, which is a renewable alternative to fossil fuels. Oil and sugars found naturally in crops like soybeans and corn are converted into liquid energy that can power both diesel- and gas-powered engines.

CHAPTER ②

The Creation of Bioproducts

Although energy is the most prominent, or widely known, application, there are plenty of other uses for renewable resources. Bioproducts are items made with natural, renewable substances. They replace similar items that are usually made with nonrenewable resources, mainly fossil fuels and minerals. Plastic is a good example of a product made with nonrenewable petroleum that can be made with renewable resources instead, such as vegetable and plant oil, cornstarch, and soybeans.

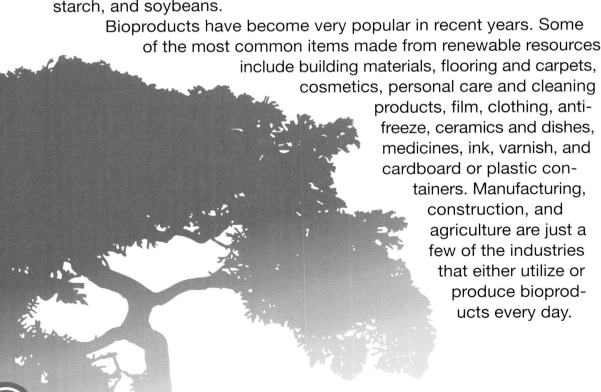

Bioproducts have become very popular in recent years. Some of the most common items made from renewable resources include building materials, flooring and carpets, cosmetics, personal care and cleaning products, film, clothing, antifreeze, ceramics and dishes, medicines, ink, varnish, and cardboard or plastic containers. Manufacturing, construction, and agriculture are just a few of the industries that either utilize or produce bioproducts every day.

RENEWABLY RAW

Just about every product begins with raw source material. "Raw" means that a substance is in its most natural form and hasn't been changed in any way. Trees, living plants, and biomass are the most common renewable raw materials used to make bioproducts. The reason for this is that vegetation contains many different natural chemicals and chemical compounds that can be extracted (pulled out), combined, and processed to make a wide variety of products.

Among the chemical compounds found in plants and crops is starch, a carbohydrate that helps plants store food. The main characteristic of starch, from a chemical standpoint, is that it binds with water to make materials thicker and bulkier. Carbohydrates are typically converted to various types of sugar, such as glucose and fructose. Sugars are important in the production of biofuels, such as ethanol.

Like starch, cellulose acts as a thickener but is mostly known for its ability to bind fluids together, even those that usually do not mix well, such as oil and water. Tape, glue, and other adhesives are made from cellulose. Found in the lining of plant cells, cellulose also produces fibers that can be twisted together to make strong thread and yarn, which can be used to create fabric. Treating cellulose fibers with tannins, which are chemical compounds found in flowering plants and tree bark, protects the fabric from falling apart as it gets older. Tannins also help natural dyes, taken from plant stems and flowers, stick better to fibers and fabric.

Proteins bind very well to other proteins, which makes them excellent adhesives. Fatty acids make plant oils more slippery than sticky, so they are mainly used as industrial lubricants, which keep machine parts from rubbing against each other. Plant oil is also a crucial ingredient in making a number of bioproducts, including biofuel and natural plastics.

POLYMERS: THE CHAINS THAT BIND

Nearly everything in the universe is made up of matter, which is any substance that has weight and takes up space. All matter contains molecules, or tiny groups of atoms held together by a combination of chemicals. Individually, these chemicals are known as monomers. When hundreds or thousands of monomers link together in a chain, they are called polymers. Scientists often use the term "polymers" to describe the various substances that make up bioproducts.

Polymers give matter bulk and shape. Think of them as LEGO building blocks. How you snap the blocks together determines the shape of whatever object you're trying to build. The same concept happens with polymers. What form matter takes depends on how the molecules of a polymer chain are linked together.

HEAT AND PRESSURE

Renewable resources must be processed in some way before they are made into environmentally sound materials and products. The goal of processing is to break down vegetation or biomass into individual, pure chemical compounds that can be extracted and used in different combinations. These new combinations produce materials that have the properties, or characteristics, of each chemical involved.

High temperatures can break down chemical compounds. With heat processing, known as distillation, biomass is essentially "cooked" in large vats at temperatures that reach upward of 392°F (200°C). The heat turns solid biomass into a gas, or vapor. This vapor

The chemical compounds in processed vegetation can be rearranged and molded to create Earth-friendly plastic containers, among other items.

is captured and cooled in another vat. Then, it is condensed, which means it's turned into a liquid. Chemical components have different boiling points, which is when steam occurs. So, they turn to vapor one at a time. Once the vapors from one chemical are collected and condensed, the remaining biomass is heated at increasingly higher temperatures until all the chemicals have been individually steamed out of the material.

Heat makes solid biomass soft and manageable, which allows natural chemicals to be more easily extracted through pressure methods like milling. Crops like corn, soy, and wheat are either ground, which means crushed, or chopped by milling devices. As a result, the vegetation is broken down into smaller units, making it easier to separate the chemicals housed in the various parts of the plant. Pressing is a similar process. Plants and crops are squeezed tightly to extract, or remove, liquids like juice and oil.

JUST ADD WATER . . . AND ENZYMES

Sometimes, other substances need to be added in order to process biomass or vegetation. One of the simplest additions is water. Hydrolysis is when water molecules break down chemical compounds into even smaller components. The hydrogen and oxygen molecules in water attach to certain chemicals and separate them from each other, thus breaking the chemical bonds of the larger compound. The process is similar to milling, except hydrolysis uses a chemical reaction instead of the physical force of crushing.

Other additives that create a chemical reaction are not as appetizing as water. For instance, bacteria or a fungus growing on a food source doesn't sound very appealing, does it? Yet, when it comes to the chemical reaction known as fermentation, these tiny living organisms mixing with vegetation is the only method to use.

Fermentation is the breakdown of natural sugars stored in plant cells. Bacteria or fungi are mixed with crushed agricultural

Ethanol, a popular alternative fuel, gets its power from a simple ear of corn. One bushel of corn can produce nearly 3 gallons (11 liters) of ethanol.

vegetation—usually corn or some kind of grain, such as wheat—in a large vat, where they feed on starch and convert it to sugar. As they eat and grow, these organisms release carbon dioxide as a waste product. Both the carbon dioxide and the sugars can be converted into energy in the form of an alcohol called ethanol. Fermentation also is responsible for the creation of several different types of food additives, or edible chemical compounds that make food look and taste better. Additives like citric acid, monosodium glutamate (MSG), and xanthan gum are made from fermented dextrose, which is a natural sugar found in animal and plant tissue.

Finally, fermenting corn releases lactic acid molecules. When linked together, these molecules form pellets of biodegradable plastic, which are molded together to make anything from containers and packing materials to clothing and textile fibers.

CHAPTER 3

Examining the Issues

When you're trying to make a decision about any situation, it's helpful to step back and look at the big picture. Too narrow a viewpoint won't give you the facts necessary to make smart choices. As you investigate the options concerning natural resources, you'll discover that there are a number of issues to consider, and some of the information is complex. Don't let that scare you. By understanding a few basic ecological concepts—overconsumption, conservation, and sustainability—and learning a bit about the pros and cons related to renewable resource use, you will ultimately make good choices.

MORE IS NOT NECESSARILY BETTER

Steady use of natural resources is to be expected. After all, humans would not be able to survive without them. Because they are slow to replenish, renewable

Lots of people use up a great deal of resources. Overpopulation, particularly when concentrated in large cities, is a major source of resource overconsumption.

resources are in danger of being used up, even under normal circumstances. Imagine what would happen if people got greedy or just didn't care, and they used more than they needed.

Unfortunately, you don't have to use your imagination. People all over the world are guilty of abusing natural resources through what's known as overconsumption. To "consume" means to use. Overconsumption, then, is using too much, beyond what is necessary. Based on scientific data collected over several decades, the WWF (formerly known as the World Wildlife Fund) estimates that worldwide consumption of natural resources has more than tripled since 1961.

The group also stated, in its 2008 "Living Planet Report," that by 2050, people will be using twice as much timber, fresh water, and other resources as Earth is able to renew. In other words, it would take two planets to meet the human demand for natural resources.

One of the reasons for runaway natural resource consumption is overpopulation. Simply put, more people living on the planet results in more resources being used. Another cause is the fact that natural resources represent a unique business opportunity. Demand for the energy and goods produced by renewable and nonrenewable resources is high. There is a lot of money to be made by whoever controls timber, oil, coal, and other resources. The chance to make huge profits can lead to natural resource exploitation, which means misuse for selfish reasons.

Perhaps the most damaging source of overconsumption is that people, especially Americans, have gotten into a consumer mentality. People in the United States tend to consume materials carelessly and worry later about the cost, whether it is money or used-up resources. Buying stuff or using resources without thinking about true need is the behavior of someone with a consumer mentality. So is wasting natural resources merely because it is cheaper or more convenient than the alternative. For instance, people might consume unnecessary amounts of oil, natural gas, or electricity because they would rather crank up the heat in their home than put on a sweater.

OVERCOMING OVERCONSUMPTION WITH CONSERVATION

Throughout the 1800s, the United States expanded westward. Hundreds of settlers arrived to find land that was unspoiled and full of natural resources. However, the supply of raw materials decreased quickly as people used plenty of timber, land, water, coal, and minerals to build and maintain their homes, farms, and towns. By the end of the nineteenth century, America had begun waking up to the fact that the

Organizations like the California Conservation Corps make it their business to help communities protect their natural resources.

country's beautiful wilderness, and all the natural resources contained within it, would not be around forever. The conservation movement was born.

Conservation involves protecting the environment by carefully managing how natural resources are used. Keeping an eye on natural resources is the job of the government and independent nonprofit groups at the national and local levels. Families and individuals can also conserve whatever resources they possess through personal property ownership. They can also join organizations that protect community-based resources.

Since forbidding all usage of natural resources isn't a practical solution, conservationists—people who practice conservation—try to find a balance between human needs and the planet's well-being. Methods designed to conserve nonrenewable resources generally revolve around reducing their use and/or finding alternate materials or forms of energy. Because nonrenewable resources are finite, meaning that they will eventually run out, the goal is to buy humans more time and stall resource depletion (reduction).

THE CASE FOR SUSTAINABILITY

Being able to use renewable resources to make lives better while still keeping the supply at reasonable, consistent levels is what's known as sustainability. Based on the idea that you don't take more than you need from the environment, sustainable development is an attempt to let humans help themselves while helping the planet.

Sustainable consumption is the opposite of overconsumption. Consuming with a purpose and according to need—not simply out of want—is the main principle of sustainable consumption. Two actions that can also make a difference are reducing the amount of resources used and keeping an eye toward replacing what is taken. In other words, you want to think about what you're using and why, and limit the amount of natural resources needed to accomplish any task.

An Astroturf-covered car certainly sends a green message. But living sustainably, by reusing vegetable oil to fuel that car, is a much more effective renewable resource choice.

Because there is an emphasis on meeting future needs, sustainable consumption benefits from planning. By thinking ahead, people can make sustainability efforts last as long as the renewable resources they are trying to protect and support—indefinitely.

RESOURCE CONSIDERATIONS

The choices that people make regarding the use of resources have far-reaching consequences. Obviously, there is the matter of exhausting resources. But there are also major environmental considerations

GREEN MEANS MONEY

It's an interesting contradiction that renewable resources—the sun, wind, and water—are available free of charge. Yet, the power and products they provide don't come cheap at all. On average, renewable energy and bioproducts cost more than their nonrenewable counter-parts. The difference is that although raw renewable materials are inexpensive, the collection methods and conversion technology can be pricey.

Cost alone should not keep you and your family from choosing renewable resources, though. Consider that most green technology is still relatively new. As humans develop better processes for capture and production, the cost will go down. In the meantime, rest assured that investing in renewable resources is a smart decision.

associated with resource choice. Countless scientific studies have concluded that nonrenewable resources, especially fossil fuels, are big-time polluters. Greenhouse gas emissions that cause global warming, water and air pollution, waste buildup in landfills, and the destruction of wildlife habitats are prime examples of the negative effect that nonrenewable resources can have on the planet.

While renewable resources are generally cleaner and cause less damage, there are still environmental concerns regarding their production and use. For instance, people are concerned because a number of birds have died after accidentally flying into the blades of wind turbines. The damming of water to generate hydropower can flood riverbanks, which can ruin the living space of fish, plants, and wild animals. The migration patterns of many fish can be obstructed as well. Dams block their path upstream to spawn (or lay eggs), and the young fish returning downstream are at risk of being sucked through turbines and killed.

Another example involves producing ethanol fuel from starchy biomass and crops, such as corn and wheat. The demand for fuel is likely to remain high no matter what the source. To meet an increased demand for ethanol, crop harvests would need to be sidetracked for fuel production, or more corn and wheat would have to be grown specifically for conversion. Either way, the concern is that more precious farmland would be dedicated to growing crops for fuel instead of producing food for humans.

A SOURCE OF CONFLICT

Resource use is politically and socially charged. Wars and other conflicts have begun over the ownership of natural resources, both renewable and nonrenewable. As Canada's International Development Research Centre and the U.S. Agency for International Development have noted, fighting over resources is fairly common. Syria and Israel had armed battles over water in the 1950s and 1960s, and violence over timber rights in Asia is an ongoing problem.

Governmental policies on the use of natural resources have been a source of tension within countries and between nations. As reported in the (Saskatoon) *StarPhoenix* in December 2005, a proposal to run a natural gas pipeline through an undeveloped section of Canada's Northwest Territories sparked great debate about federal investment in renewable, as opposed to nonrenewable, resources. Heated debate continues within the United States over whether or not the country should drill for oil in the Alaskan wilderness and off the shores of the U.S. coastline. America's refusal to sign the 1997 Kyoto Protocol, an international agreement to reduce greenhouse gas emissions and invest in renewable resources, still disappoints and angers many in the global community.

On a personal level, people have been mocked, criticized, and even harassed for their personal beliefs regarding natural resource use. People who are skeptical about global warming or careless with nonrenewable resources tend to laugh off the concerns of those who worry about the environment. The way to overcome tension created by a disagreement like this is to respect the choices of those who think differently, just as you would like them to respect your outlook and decisions.

MYTHS AND
FACTS
MYTHS AND FACTS
MYTHS AND
FACTS
MYTHS A

MYTHS
AND FACTS MYTHS AND
FACTS
MYTHS
FAC

MYTH: The amount of power generated by alternative energy sources is minute and couldn't possibly meet American energy needs.

FACT: The U.S. Department of Energy (DOE) estimates that wind power collected in North Dakota, Kansas, and Texas alone could generate even more electricity than the entire nation currently consumes. DOE research also indicates that solar power collected from 100 square miles (259 sq kilometers) in the Nevada desert has the same potential. A commitment to collecting and using alternative energy is what seems to be lacking.

MYTH: Solar energy relies on heat to generate electricity, so cities in colder climates cannot use it.

FACT: Light, not heat, is what makes solar energy possible. Any location that receives a decent amount of sunlight can use solar energy.

MYTH: The supply of renewable resources is endless, no matter how people use them.

FACT: People should not use resources faster than those resources can renew themselves. Renewable resources can go on indefinitely, but only if humans give them time to renew or replace themselves.

CHAPTER 4

Renew at School

Now that you're familiar with the many choices available for renewable resource use, it's time to discover how to put your choices into action. School is an excellent place to demonstrate your commitment to renewable resources for a number of reasons. First, school campuses contain several different areas—classrooms, auditorium, cafeteria, and library—that serve particular purposes. Each location has specific energy and material needs, so you can introduce a wide mix of renewable products under one roof.

Second, teachers who conduct classes in science, ecology, or other related subjects are available to answer any questions that you might have about making green choices. Their knowledge of renewable resources might influence you to make additional choices that you may not have considered before. Also, you will need the support and guidance of adults for some of the activities suggested in this chapter.

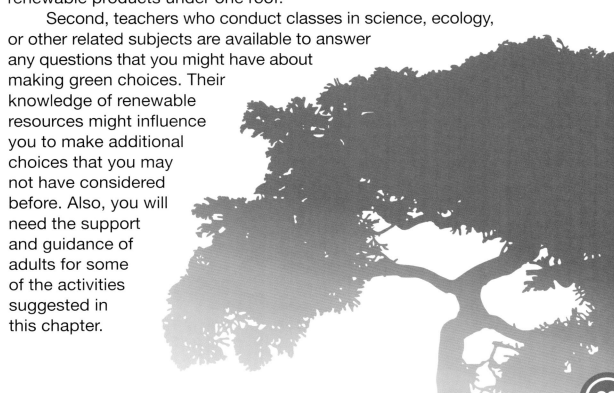

Last, schools can supply one of the most valuable renewable resources ever—your classmates. When you come together with like-minded people, those who think the way you do and have made many of the same choices, there's no telling what great things you can accomplish.

THE WRITE STUFF

The school administration puts you on a schedule of classes, and the state determines what must be covered in required courses. But you pretty much have absolute control over the type of supplies that you use. With a bit of investigating, you can find equipment made from renewable resources.

Pencils are an easy choice. They are made from wood, which is renewable. Taking the concept a step further, there are pencil manufacturers that claim to use only wood from what they call "renewable forests." A renewable forest is a wooded area that is under sustainable management, which helps guarantee that a roughly equal number of trees will be grown to replace those that are cut down for timber.

To correct mistakes made with renewable pencils, try using a natural rubber eraser. Most erasers these days are made from synthetic (man-made) materials, not latex, which is a natural rubber. Be careful; if you are allergic to latex, you shouldn't use natural rubber erasers.

The growing number of plastic products made from renewable resources includes pens. Corn bioplastic forms the barrels, or hard shells, of some renewable pens. Other manufacturers, such as Bic, convert wood pulp into material that can be molded and shaped. So far, the ink in pens is still petroleum-based. But the full-color sections of around 90 percent of U.S. newspapers, including USA Today, are printed using ink that's made from a mix of soybeans and a tiny bit of petroleum (added to help the ink dry quickly). Perhaps someday soon, pen ink will be made from renewable resources, too.

Only timber products from sustainable forests earn the U.S. Forest Stewardship Council's seal of approval. Consumers should look for "FSC" to be certain.

Tree pulp is also used to make the paper in notebooks. So is biomass from banana, papaya, and coconut trees, as well as bamboo, hemp, and other plant fibers. Even rocks have been ground and grated into chalk powder to make paper. However, these tree-free papers are not widely available. Your best bet for taking notes and writing reports on paper made from renewable resources may be the regular wood-pulp kind. The U.S. Forest Stewardship Council, an organization that oversees sustainable forest management practices, recommends buying products made from trees grown specifically for papermaking, marked "FSC" on the label. You earn extra environmental points if the

GREAT QUESTIONS TO ASK A
SCIENCE TEACHER

TEN

 1. What are the major benefits of using renewable energy and bioproducts?

 2. What countries use the most renewable resources, and which use the least?

 3. Which is the most efficient form of renewable energy, and why?

 4. What classroom experiments best demonstrate how renewable energy works?

 5. How do scientists determine the rate at which renewable resources replenish (renew) themselves?

 6. Why does it sometimes cost more, in terms of money and energy, to use renewable resources?

 7. What are some of the new technologies being researched that could make renewable resources easier to tap and use in the future?

 8. What renewable resources do you use on a regular basis, and why?

 9. What would you suggest I do to help conserve natural resources?

 10. Will you help me lead efforts to make our school a greener place through renewable resource use?

sheets in your notebook have recycled material in the mix. The paper will be marked "PCW," which stands for Post Consumer Waste.

STICK TO IT OR BAG IT

Creating artwork, putting together displays, or merely hanging pictures in your locker can become a green experience when you use adhesives made from renewable materials. Cellulose-based tape is transparent and doesn't get that yellow cloudiness as it ages. Although it has mostly industrial uses, such as securing cardboard packages, cellulose tape comes in a variety of widths, including the standard size found in tape dispensers.

Natural glue sticks are made by mixing starches and sugars, as well as other organic and sticky ingredients like tapioca. They're effective on paper, wood, and fabric.

Biobased glue sticks are harder to come by than cellulose tape. Natural adhesives are commonly used in construction and to hold wood products together. Not many manufacturers produce organic glues for use in the classroom or at home.

Once you've gathered all your renewable supplies, you will need an environmentally conscious way to cart them to school. Totes and backpacks made from renewable fabrics, such as organic cotton or hemp, are popular choices these days. There are even messenger bags and backpacks outfitted with solar panels. Using a built-in adapter, these solar bags are capable of recharging small electronics like cell phones and MP3 players. Some even offer battery packs that store energy for use when the sun goes down. Most solar bags are made from recycled plastic soda bottles.

WORK TO ECO-ENERGIZE YOUR SCHOOL

You might not have the vaguest notion about how to put in solar panels or erect a wind turbine, but there are other ways to bring renewable

RENEWABLE ENERGY REWARDS

Largely because of the technology involved, wind and solar electricity costs more to produce than traditional power from fossil fuels. The production costs paid by energy providers are passed on to consumers. The possibility of paying higher energy bills can keep schools from investing in renewable power.

Yet in many cases, states offer incentives to customers who purchase renewable energy. Incentives for buying renewable electricity may include cash back or tax breaks. For instance, according to the Sierra Student Coalition, a division of the Sierra Club environmental organization, New Jersey refunds up to 60 percent of the cost to install solar power technology.

Investigate what incentives are available in your area. North Carolina State University's Solar Center posts a database of renewable energy incentive programs by state at http://www.dsireusa.org.

energy to your school. You will have to do a little extra homework to make this happen. Dividing up the work by making the task a group project for your friends and classmates is a smart idea.

The first step is to find out what company your school buys its electricity from. You can ask the facility manager, who oversees the crew that maintains the building and grounds, for this information. Also ask if your school currently uses renewable energy, either in part or entirely, and what the source of that energy is—wind, solar, etc.

Chances are that your school purchases energy from a local provider. Next, go online to the provider's Web site, or call the company's

Solar panels on backpacks don't make students' loads any lighter. Yet, they do keep personal electronics powered up and ready to go.

customer service department, to discover what renewable energy plans are available to commercial customers. Compare what the provider offers with the plan that your school currently uses. Collect information on any plan or program that offers more renewable or alternative forms of energy than the school is already using.

Next, you need to talk to the facility manager and administrators about the school's energy purchases. Show these people what you have learned about renewable energy options. Explain how beneficial using alternative energy is, not only to the environment but also to humans. In a professional, knowledgeable manner, try to convince them that the school should be using as much energy from renewable resources as possible.

Newer schools are built with energy efficiency in mind, as shown by the partial underground construction seen here in Boise, Idaho. Even older schools can make and implement green choices, though.

"LEARN, EXPLORE, ACT"

Firsthand experience, in which you learn by doing, is the idea behind several environmental programs designed for students. Some are regionally or nationally based, while others have an international scope. Participation in these programs can increase your knowledge about renewable resources and other environmental issues, introduce you to like-minded students outside your classroom, and motivate you to take action.

The Northeast Sustainable Energy Association offers many programs that are open to students in New England and the Mid-Atlantic states. The organization's Clean, Green Power Project uses a three-step

This teen participates in the Wind Wisdom Group, a special program made available to Girl Scouts in Massachusetts. The Girl Scouts meet with wind energy professionals to learn about wind as a renewable resource.

plan. In step one, you learn about green power, which is produced by renewable resources, and then you test your knowledge through quizzes and surveys. Step two has you explore clean energy options in your area through visits and interviews. Finally, step three involves sharing what you have learned through the creation of a science, communication, or art project. Completion of all three steps earns you a certificate and/or a Girl Scout badge.

The association's Wind Wisdom Program offers several activities, administered by your teacher, which emphasize the importance of wind power. You can receive a certificate and a Girl Scout badge after successfully taking part in at least four of the listed activities.

The Sierra Student Coalition sponsors the Campus Climate Challenge, a national project aimed at reducing energy use and America's dependence on fossil fuels. Students challenge themselves, classmates, and administrators to use clean, renewable energy throughout their school's buildings and grounds in the hope of reducing global warming. Guidelines are available on the Sierra Student Coalition's Web site, http://www.ssc.org/climate.

Students from around the world participate in My Community, Our Earth. Also known as MyCOE, the program provides resources and mentors to help young adults of all nationalities carry out local sustainability projects. There is no cost to join or to suggest a project of your own. For online information, see http://www.aag.org/sustainable.

CHAPTER 5

Good Choices for You and Your Home

How people choose to decorate their homes and dress themselves is an expression of their personal style. The energy they use to heat and light their homes and the fabrics their clothes are made of represent their resource-use style.

Many different types of renewable energy and bioproducts are available for personal and home use. In fact, because so many consumers are requesting—even demanding—renewable materials, more manufacturers are developing green alternatives to their usual mineral- and fossil fuel–based offerings at a rapid pace. All it takes to make renewables a part of your life is some research and the willingness to seek out companies that can deliver the green goods.

HOME ENERGY USAGE

Perhaps the most obvious way to bring renewable resources into your home is to

Manufacturers are producing smaller, affordable versions of alternative energy collectors, such as this turbine meant for home use.

use alternative energy to heat your living space and water tank, as well as to power electric gadgets and appliances. Your local energy provider undoubtedly has a plan that allows customers to purchase wind, solar, or hydropower. If your family is not currently taking advantage of these plans, talk to your parents. Share with them the advantages of using renewable energy—it's clean and good for the environment—and urge them to switch to a greener power source.

If you have the time and the money, you can also take matters into your own hands by placing renewable energy devices throughout your home. Many manufacturers of solar panels and wind turbines make and install small home-use versions of their products. (Keep in mind

WHAT A LITTLE JUNK AND CREATIVITY CAN DO

If you're a fan of the television show *Extreme Makeover: Home Edition*, you might be familiar with the story of Garrett Yazzie. He and his family had been living in a mobile home with no central heating system. Fumes from the coal stove they had been using to keep warm made his sister sick.

So, Yazzie built a solar-powered house and water heater using a bunch of recycled soda cans, an old car radiator, Plexiglas, and other materials that he found in a junkyard. He was only thirteen years old at the time. The homemade heater earned him a trip to the Discovery Channel Young Scientist Challenge in 2007, where he placed seventh out of forty finalists.

Members of the *Extreme Makeover* cast were so impressed with Yazzie's work that they saved the solar panel and hung it as artwork in his family's new house.

that your family must own a fairly large piece of land in order to build a turbine for home use.) If you try to convince your parents to go this route, they will, of course, ask about the price. You should be prepared with some facts and figures.

The American Wind Energy Association estimates that home-use, or residential, turbines run between $6,000 and $22,000 installed (set up). That's a serious investment of cash. But you should point out to your folks that, on average, residential turbine owners save at least 50 percent on their electricity bill, according to the association.

A July 17, 2008, CNN report stated that the average cost of home solar systems was about $12,000. Do-it-yourselfers can purchase renewable energy kits and small, individual solar panels at home improvement and electronics stores, or through online distributors, for less. The *Los Angeles Times* reported in May 2007 that active solar-powered water heaters alone can cost anywhere from $4,000 to $6,000. According to the Texas State Energy Conservation Office, water heaters that use passive solar heat sell for $800 to $1,500, but do-it-yourselfers who build their own often wind up paying under $400 for materials.

SIMPLER HOME-BASED IDEAS

Getting the benefits of renewable energy doesn't have to be complicated or bust your family's budget. Plenty of simple actions—some of which you may already do without even thinking about them—also support your renewable lifestyle.

Some manufacturers of laundry detergents boast that their products can give your clothes the scent of sunshine and fresh spring breezes. Why not get that scent the natural way and boost your commitment to using renewable resources at the same time? Hanging wet laundry outside to dry is low-tech and maybe a little old-fashioned. Yet, it is also a smart move away from dependence on nonrenewable coal or natural gas, which power most clothes dryers.

To raise temperatures in your home, leave curtains open during the day so that rooms can absorb passive solar energy. On the other hand, closing shades or drapes helps to lower temperatures naturally. Window awnings and materials that reflect sunlight, such as metal or tile roofs and light-colored paint, can also cause a cooling effect. Even merely opening windows to get a breeze is a great renewable alternative to running the air conditioning or plugging in electric fans.

Another renewable heating option that people may take for granted is fueled by wood. Burning logs has been a source of warmth

Insulating your home—especially with modern materials made from renewable fibers, like sheep's wool—saves heat, money, and the environment.

since prehistoric days. Modern technology has made fire more efficient and effective. Today's fireplaces are built to generate as much heat as ever but use less wood, saving you money as well as trees for the future. If your house has a wood stove or a wood-burning fireplace, use it often. Even better, attach a blower that distributes hot air more thoroughly. Look for stoves that have been certified by the Environmental Protection Agency (EPA) and have fireplace inserts, which cut down on the smoke produced by burning wood.

You and your family can keep more of that fireplace heat inside your home by insulating your attic with renewable materials. Instead of pink synthetic fiberglass, which is the most common form of

Solar cookers can be as low-tech as cardboard lined with aluminum foil. Plans for more elaborate models can be found on the Internet.

insulation, try laying down a layer of sheep's wool called Thermafleece. Other materials that you may use include sheets of hemp-based Natilin or Warmcell rolls, which are created from recycled newspaper.

NOW YOU'RE (SOLAR) COOKING!

If someone in your family is comfortable whipping up meals using a slow cooker, he or she might like to try solar cooking. Both methods heat food slowly. With solar cooking, sunlight passes through the glass lid of a shallow box that has a shiny, reflective inner surface. Once inside, the sun's rays heat the box and the pot filled with food that is placed inside. Solar cooking pots are painted dark colors so that they can absorb more heat.

Solar cookers are left out in the sun for hours at a time, but temperatures don't get very high. The longer cooking time makes up for the lower heat. Obviously, how well solar cooking works for you will depend on the amount of sun that shines where you live.

Cooking with solar heat will never take the place of using conventional ovens. Still, it's fun to experiment with solar cooking occasionally. Building your own solar cooker is fairly easy. All you need is a couple of cardboard boxes, aluminum foil, a piece of glass, black paint, and some glue. Instructions on how to put these materials together, as well as cooking times for certain foods, can be found on the Internet. For example, the NASA Langley Research Center's instructions are at http://scifiles.larc.nasa.gov/text/educators/ activities/2000_2001/inclass/solar_cooker.html. Various cookers also appear at http://www.solarcooking.org/plans.

BECOME A RENEWABLE CONSUMER

Every time you open your wallet, you have the opportunity to make a strong statement about renewable resource use. Choosing to buy items made with renewable resources, which are commonly called

This high school student participates in a model solar car race held in Green Bay, Wisconsin. Students learn to create devices with a solar theme to test their knowledge of solar renewable energy.

"green" or "eco-friendly," means checking labels and considering the source of the ingredients or contents listed there.

Clothes are a good place to start. Choose natural fabrics, such as cotton and wool, which are renewable. Cotton is made from crops that can be replanted each season, and wool grows back after it has been clipped off of sheep. Synthetics, on the other hand, are polymers made from mixing manufactured chemicals and nonrenewable resources, such as petroleum, coal, or tar. Nylon, polyester, Spandex, and acrylic are synthetic fabrics.

An assortment of personal care and beauty products also makes the most of renewable resources. Lotions, soaps, shampoo, toothpaste, and cosmetics are some of the items that traditionally have contained nonrenewable substances or chemical compounds. But they are increasingly being made from renewable sources. Check the labels of these products. The more recognizable the ingredients are, the better.

Cleaning solutions are another area where you can exercise your choice of renewable consuming. Look for the U.S. Department of Agriculture's "Certified Organic" seal, which guarantees that the products are made primarily from natural and renewable resources. "Organic" is the word that you should look for in produce as well. Few to no chemicals and pesticides are added to food that is grown organically. That means there is much less chance that the soil in which organic crops are grown will be contaminated and become toxic. The purer the soil, the longer it can be used to produce healthy, renewable food products.

Where you and your family buy products also has an impact. Giving your business only to manufacturers and stores that have a wide selection of green merchandise sends a message to other retailers that they need to offer more items made from renewable resources or risk losing money. That includes groceries. Buy food at cooperative and natural food stores, or from local farms and farm markets. More organic items are stocked in these locations.

GIVE YOUR CHOICE A VOICE

The choices you make when it comes to using renewable resources at home are up to you. But what about the choices that other people make? You can't, and shouldn't, force anyone to make the same decisions that you do. However, you might be able to influence or inspire someone to see your side of the story by becoming an advocate.

Someone who believes in a cause so strongly that he or she can't help but speak out is an advocate. Being an advocate for renewable resources first and foremost involves sharing what you know about their use. Talk to your friends and family, create a presentation, or write a letter to the editor of your local paper about the importance of conservation and sustainable consumption.

Following the idea that actions speak louder than words, you should also lead by example. Make it a habit to use bioproducts and renewable energy every chance you get. Acting on your decision to use renewable resources is the surest way to prove—to others and yourself—that you have made the right choice.

additives Substances added to improve food, such as its flavor, appearance, or shelf-life.

biomass The scientific name for organic plant material and waste matter.

cellulose A carbohydrate found in the lining of plant cells.

condenser A machine that uses pressure to turn heated water into vapor.

conservation Protection of the environment through careful management of how natural resources are used.

consumption The use of a resource.

distillation The process of heating a substance and collecting the vapor that results.

ethanol An alcohol obtained from the fermentation plant sugars and starches that can be used as biofuel.

fermentation The breakdown of natural sugars that are stored in plant cells.

fossil fuels Fuels like coal, oil, and natural gas that have been formed over millions of years from the remains of ancient plants and animals.

geothermal Relating to Earth's internal heat.

habitat The place in an ecosystem where an organism lives.

hydrolysis The process in which water molecules break down chemical compounds into even smaller components.

hydropower Electricity that is generated by the power of moving water.

impoundment The creation of a body of water by damming.

incentive Something that encourages or motivates someone to do something.

insulation A nonconducting material that is placed around something in order to protect it from heat, cold, or noise.

kinetics Movement by force.

lactic acid A human-made form of a compound that is used as a flavoring and preservative in foods and beverages.

organic Relating to material made of or by living organisms or once-living organisms.

parabolic A curved shape resting on a flat plane.

photovoltaic Having the ability to produce energy (volts) when exposed to light.

polymers A chain of thousands of chemicals that give matter bulk and shape.

renewable Having the ability to be replaced by new growth.

sustainability The use of resources to make people's lives better while still keeping the supply at reasonable, consistent levels.

technology The study, development, and application of devices, machines, and methods for manufacturing and other processes.

turbine A machine or motor that creates electricity by using kinetics.

FOR MORE INFORMATION

Alliance to Save Energy
1850 M Street NW, Suite 600
Washington, DC 20036
(202) 857-0666
Web site: http://www.ase.org/section/_audience/consumers/kids
The Alliance to Save Energy is a nonprofit group that offers informa-
    tion and educational programs on reducing greenhouse gas
    emissions and saving consumers money.

Earthwatch Institute
3 Clock Tower Place, Suite 100
Box 75
Maynard, MA 01754
(800) 776-0188
Earthwatch Institute is an international nonprofit organization that gives
    people the opportunity to join scientific research teams around the
    world. This firsthand experience promotes the understanding and
    action necessary to achieve a sustainable environment.

Environment Canada
70 Crémazie Street
Gatineau, QC K1A 0H3
Canada
(800) 668-6767 (Canada only)
(819) 997-2800
Web site: http://www.ec.gc.ca
Environment Canada's mission is to preserve and enhance the quality
    of the natural environment and conserve Canada's renewable
    resources.

Natural Resources Canada
Renewable and Electrical Energy Division
Ottawa, ON K1A 0J9
Canada
(613) 995-0947
Web site: http://www2.nrcan.gc.ca/es/erb/erb/english/View.asp?x=68
The Renewable and Electrical Energy division provides information on
    renewable energy technologies in Canada and promotes invest-
    ments in renewable energy systems for heating and cooling.

Renewable Natural Resources Foundation
5430 Grosvenor Lane
Bethesda, MD 20814-2142
(301) 493-9101
Web site: http://www.rnrf.org
The Renewable Natural Resources Foundation provides information
    regarding the application of sound and promotes scientific
    practices in managing and conserving renewable natural resources.

Renewable Resource Data Center
1617 Cole Boulevard
Golden, CO 80401-3393
(303) 275-3000
Web site: http://www.nrel.gov/rredc
The Renewable Resource Data Center provides access to an extensive
    collection of renewable energy resource data, maps, and tools.

Responsible Shopper
1612 K Street NW, Suite 600

Washington, DC 20006

Web site: http://www.coopamerica.org/programs/rs

Responsible Shopper alerts the public about the social and environmental impact of major corporations and provides opportunities
for people to vote for change with their dollars.

Sierra Student Coalition

600 Fourteenth Street NW, Suite 750

Washington, DC 20005

(888) 564-6722

Web site: http://www.ssc.org

An offshoot of the Sierra Club, the Sierra Student Coalition trains
and organizes high school and college students from across
the United States to be leaders in the fight to protect the
environment. The SSC offers information on how to make
your school green by using renewable resources, including
sample petitions.

U.S. Department of Energy

1000 Independence Avenue SW

Washington, DC 20585

(800) 342-5363

Web site: http://www.energy.gov

The Department of Energy's Office of Energy Efficiency and Renewable
Energy sponsors various initiatives to build awareness about energy
efficiency and renewable energy topics.

U.S. Environmental Protection Agency

Ariel Rios Building

1200 Pennsylvania Avenue NW
Washington, DC 20460
Web site: http://epa.gov
The EPA works to protect human health and the environment.

U.S. Geological Survey
12201 Sunrise Valley Drive
Reston, VA 20192
(888) 275-8747
Web site: http://www.usgs.gov
The U.S. Geological Survey provides reliable scientific information
about Earth and natural resources.

WEB SITES

Due to the changing nature of Internet links, Rosen Publishing has
developed an online list of Web sites related to the subject of this book.
This site is updated regularly. Please use this link to access the list:

http://www.rosenlinks.com/gre/rene

FOR FURTHER READING

Ball, Jacqueline A., and Paul Barnett, et al. *Conservation and Natural Resources*. Strongsville, OH: Gareth Stevens Publishing, 2004.

Bauman, Amy. *Earth's Natural Resources*. Strongsville, OH: Gareth Stevens Publishing, 2008.

Belmont, Helen. *Planning for a Sustainable Future*. North Mankato, MN: Smart Apple Media, 2007.

Parks, Peggy J. *Global Resources*. Chicago, IL: Lucent Books, 2004.

Passero, Barbara, ed. *Energy Alternatives: Opposing Viewpoints*. Farmington Hills, MI: Greenhaven Press, 2006.

Raum, Elizabeth. *Potato Clocks and Solar Cars: Renewable and Non-renewable Energy*. Chicago, IL: Heinemann-Raintree, 2007.

Simon, Christopher A. *Alternative Energy: Political, Economic, and Social Feasibility*. Lanham, MD; Rowman & Littlefield Publishers, 2006.

Sobha, Geeta. *Green Technology: Earth-Friendly Innovations*. New York, NY: Rosen Publishing, 2007.

Spilsbury, Louise. *A Sustainable Future: Saving and Recycling Resources*. Chicago, IL: Heinemann-Raintree, 2006.

Walker, Niki. *Biomass: Fueling Change*. New York, NY: Crabtree Publishing Company, 2007.

Winters, Adam. *Destruction of Earth's Resources: The Need for Sustainable Development*. New York, NY: Rosen Publishing, 2006.

BIBLIOGRAPHY

Braunegg, Gerhart, et al. "From Renewable Resources to Bulk Products: The Future Is White Biotechnology." Graz (Austria) University of Technology, May 2007. Retrieved September 30, 2008 (http://www.hdb.hr/bec2008/PDF_files/Braunegg_Bulk.pdf).

Brown, Lester R. "Want a Better Way to Power Your Car? It's a Breeze." *Washington Post*, August 31, 2008, p. B03.

Chemical Sciences Roundtable, National Research Council. *Carbon Management: Implications for R & D in the Chemical Sciences and Technology*. Washington, DC: The National Academies Press, 2001, pp. 166, 167.

CNN. "Unique Business Aims to Spread Solar Power." July 2008. Retrieved October 2008 (http://www.cnn.com/2008/TECH/07/17/solar.office/index.html?iref=mpstoryview).

Energy Canada. "Renewable Energy: Hydropower in Canada." June 2008. Retrieved September 2008 (http://www.ic.gc.ca/epic/site/rei-ier.nsf/en/h_nz00010e.html).

Energy Information Administration. "Renewable Energy Sources: A Consumer's Guide." U.S. Department of Energy, 2004. Retrieved September 30, 2008 (http://www.eia.doe.gov/neic/brochure/renew05/renewable.html).

Green Biz. "Soy What? Soy Ink Makes a Splash." July 2001. Retrieved October 13, 2008 (http://www.greenercomputing.com/news/2001/07/25/soy-what-soy-ink-makes-a-splash).

Helmenstein, Anne Marie. "What Is Distillation?" About.com. Retrieved September 30, 2008 (http://chemistry.about.com/cs/5/f/bldistillation.htm).

International Development Research Centre. "Cultivating Peace: Conflict Over Natural Resources." Retrieved October 13, 2008 (http://www.idrc.ca/CONFLICT).

Jackson, David. "Bush Calls for End to Ban on Offshore Oil Drilling."
    New York Times, June 19, 2008, p. A1.

Morgan, Sally. *Alternative Energy Sources*. Chicago, IL: Reed
    Educational and Professional Publishing/Heinemann Library, 2003.

Murphy, Dominic. "The Green Consumer: Loft Insulation." *Guardian* (UK),
    April 26, 2005, Weekend Comment & Features section, p. 69.

Orb, Jocelyn. "Leaders Ignore Canadians' Support for Kyoto
    Accord." *StarPhoenix* (Saskatoon, Saskatchewan), December 1,
    2005, p. A13.

Pahl, Greg. *The Citizen-Powered Energy Handbook: Community
    Solutions to a Global Crisis*. White River Junction, VT: Chelsea
    Green Publishing Co., 2007.

Roosevelt, Margot. "Bill Heats Up Talk of Solar Water Systems."
    Los Angeles Times, May 29, 2007, p. B-1.

Texas State Energy Conservation Office. "Solar Water Heaters."
    SECO Fact Sheet No. 10, p. 3. Retrieved October 14, 2008
    (http://www.infinitepower.org/factsheets.htm).

U.S. Agency for International Development. "Seeking Peace and
    Saving Forests: Why Should We Be Concerned?" April 2007.
    Retrieved October 13, 2008 (http://www.forestconflict.com/
    new_site/subpages/why_concerned.html).

U.S. Department of Energy. "Learning About PV: The Myths of Solar
    Electricity." July 2008. Retrieved September 30, 2008 (http://
    www1.eere.energy.gov/solar/myths.html).

WWF. "Human Footprint Too Big for Nature." October 2006.
    Retrieved September 30, 2008 (http://www.panda.org/
    index.cfm?uNewsID=83520).

INDEX

ABOUT THE AUTHOR

Jeanne Nagle is a writer and editor who lives in upstate New York. She has a long-standing interest in environmental issues and is a member of a grassroots environmental group in her area. Among the titles she has written for Rosen Publishing are *Reducing Your Carbon Footprint at School* and *Smart Shopping: Shopping Green* (Your Carbon Footprint series), and *Living Green* (In the News series).

PHOTO CREDITS

Cover, p. 1 © www.istockphoto.com/NiseriN; p. 7 © Lester Lefkowitz/Corbis; p. 8 © David Burton/Beateworks/Corbis; p. 10 (left) © www.istockphoto.com/Gene Krebs; p. 10 (right) © www.istockphoto.com/Tony Tremblay; p. 13 © Geoff Renner/Robert Harding World Imagery/Corbis; p. 14 © Everett Kennedy Brown/epa/Corbis; pp. 19, 38, 48, 50 © AP Images; p. 21 Scott Olson/Getty Images; p. 24 Mario Tama/Getty Images; p. 26 Rod Rolle/Getty Images; p. 28 Sarah Leen/National Geographic/Getty Images; p. 35 © Carlos Avila Gonzalez/San Francisco Chronicle/Corbis; p. 40 © David R. Frazier/The Image Works; p. 41 Courtesy Northeast Sustainable Energy Association; p. 44 Sipa/Newscom.com; p. 47 courtesy www.secondnatureuk.com.

Designer: Nicole Russo; Editor: Kathy Kuhtz Campbell; Photo Researcher: Amy Feinberg